THE SEVEN BODIES

OF MAN

THE

SEVEN BODIES

OF MAN

E. J. GOLD

GATEWAYS / IDHHB, INC.
PUBLISHERS

Frontispiece photo by Philip Stark, NYC

Copyright ©1989 by E.J. Gold
All Rights Reserved. Printed in the U.S.A.
First Printing.

Published by:
GATEWAYS / IDHHB, INC.
PO Box 370 Nevada City, CA 95959, (916) 477-1116

Some of the material in this book first appeared as a privately published edition, *Volume VI* of the *Secret Talks with G.* series, ©1980. Additional material has appeared in *Secret Talks on Voluntary Evolution,* ©1982.

Library of Congress Cataloging-in-Publication Data

Gold, E.J.
  The seven bodies of man / by E.J. Gold.
  p. cm.
  ISBN 0-89556-060-7 : $12.50
  1. Bodies of man (Occultism) 2. Spiritual life. I. Title.
BF1442.B63G65 1989
133—dc20   89-38914
                                                    CIP

The illustrations in *The Seven Bodies of Man* are taken from a recent series called *Planar Contiguities.* These are large-scale oil paintings by E.J. Gold. In these canvases, Gold suggests disconcerting realities, rendering subtle atmospheres and moods. He is an artist who boldly experiments with form, color, perspective and texture in such a way as to confront most perceptual and aesthetic expectations.

E.J. Gold views his studio as an alchemical laboratory. His experiments on canvas as well as in other artistic media including sculpture, printmaking, music and video, are intended to challenge ordinary assumptions, both artistic and cosmological, and open new perspectives.

Limited-edition Fine Art prints of some of the *Planar Contiguities* images included in this book as well as many other works by E.J. Gold have been published by Heidelberg Editions International and are available for purchase. Information may be obtained by writing to Gateways, PO Box 370, Nevada City, CA 95959, Telephone: (916) 477-1116.

On the Cover:

E.J. Gold, *Bright Side Crossing,* Oil on Canvas, 48" x 60", 1987.

TABLE OF CONTENTS

PREFACE

Attending a seminar on the *bhumis* of the Bhod-
hisatva path led by Chögyam Trungpa in the early
70's, I ran into Sarah Warsher—former Esalen
secretary, who had been on the verge of joining the
group I selected to come to Arica to work with
Oscar Ichazo in 1970. She had chosen to become
Fritz Perls's secretary in the end, when Fritz left
Esalen to start the "Gestalt kibbutz" in Cowichan,
and I had not seen her since. She had not found a
teacher since Fritz, she said, and I take it that she
did not become Trungpa's disciple, for, a few
weeks after our meeting, I received an enthusiastic
letter from her telling me that at last she had come
in contact with one who stood at the very core of
the School (or something like that). People at the
Gestalt Center in Cowichan had turned things over

to him and within a short time there would be a brief opening up to the community—in the form of a series of workshops by their master; soon after that, however, the group would concentrate on their own inner work, and their teacher on them. Because of that, she recommended I come to one of the scheduled events.

I chose an intensive workshop on "objective movement"—and took a plane for Vancouver at great sacrifice—at a time of exhaustion, when I could hardly cope with the five hundred students that I had come to teach directly or indirectly through "SAT" (Seekers After Truth). The workshop involved the development of an illusory time expansion by complete darkness and by the experience of being woken up at what one felt like various times in the course of the first 24 hours or so. It was also a workshop of high energy expenditure, that made me keenly aware of my limitations when it came to maintaining the "work attitude" in the midst of fatigue. It was also an event in which we, the participants, were treated as children in a kindergarten even to the point of being read (most relevant) bed time stories. But the master was not there.

Only a visiting card was to be seen on the bulletin board—a shining blue-gray visiting card at the center of which stood the name Avatar Al-Washi with a footnote in smaller writing clarifying: "worlds created, maintained and destroyed, while-u-wait" and an address on Wilshire Boulevard, L.A. I was only able to meet E.J. in person at a later event, at a time when I learnt that his students called him "Beast." This was congruent with Aleister Crowley's "Master Therion," and with the meaning of Al-Washi ("The Wild One"); but, most of all, it was congruent with a "wrathful" teaching style reminiscent of Gurdjieff's. Also reminiscent of Gurdjieff's was his shaven head. Later, I was to think, was it the shaven head of a priest or that of a Gurdjieff imitator?—and today I would answer: both: for I see in E.J. a rare (though archetypal) kind of a master who is also a joker and a juggler, and who has deliberately played Gurdjieff in addressing himself to both Gurdjieff fans and imitation-Gurdjieff teachers. As a once disciple of Gurdjieff disciples and also as a disciple of Ichazo, who was in some ways Gurdjieff's continuator, this role of E.J. was of particular importance in my own experience, both as a person and a teacher. Though I couldn't clearly appreciate it at the time, too, his enactment of a wild Avatar role was most appropriate to my situation at a time when I felt somewhat messianic and my teaching style had become demanding and critical in the name of "ego-reduction."

Soon after my second visit to Cowichan, I received a phone call from Sarah conveying E.J. Gold's offer (this was the first time I knew his name) to meet with my students in Berkeley over a weekend so as to direct them to the next stage in their path.

"How many can he see?" I asked. — Any number.

I proposed a session with a group of 90 and then individual sessions with each, wondering how he would do it (and not trusting him enough to introduce him to more than two of the five ongoing groups in town). E.J. did see everybody in less than a day—sometimes in interviews no longer than a minute, leaving significant impressions on many. Yet more important to me was what transpired when, before visiting my students and immediately after his arrival he walked into my room with a tape-recorder identical to the rather unusual one that I had purchased the day before. He played for me a number of tapes (including the parody of an Olympic competition in which various spiritual leaders of the day gained or lost precedence*). After listening to these tapes, and after he left, I realized that he had managed to transpose his machine with mine; where I had been sitting (and connected to my loud-speakers!) was a machine not quite identical to mine, for it differed from it in that it had been banged to a point of not looking very new at all. I couldn't believe, when I discovered this, that he could be such a "Beast",— a being of such an aggressive energy that he could have impinged so destructively on my tape-recorder without my even noticing it. On studying the matter more closely, however, I afterwards discovered the brand new machine in *his* place,

* Editor's Note: This tape has recently been re-released by Gateways under the title, *Hi-Tech Shaman at the Spiritual Olympics*.

connected to *his* portable speakers. At first I could not bring myself to believe that he could have exchanged his old machine for my new one—but one detail gave me the proof: inside the battery compartment stood a label bearing the name of the store in Oakland where I had purchased it. It angered me, and it seems that I was not ready to give away my beautiful and rare stereo cassette recorder with its appealing three-fold design (though years later I was to donate it to H.H. Karmapa). In spite of feeling angry and of thinking that, if he had not precisely ruined my new cassette recorder, he had, in a subtle way, attempted to steal it, I didn't find it easy to reciprocate by switching the machines back. Or, rather: I did, but felt like a thief in doing so.

Sometime during the following day "Mr. Gold" invited me to hear a cassette, and had his machine brought to where we were sitting. The tape was not of particular interest, and the point of the episode was an implicit confrontation of the tape-recorder issue and my good-boyish fear of facing the powerful master. He acknowledged it obliquely when he said, at the time of saying good-bye immediately afterwards—"We did a good piece of work, there, didn't we?"

My next encounter with "E.J." (as I called him by then) took place perhaps a year after this, when he and his community had migrated to the Crestline mountains in Southern California. There I was invited one day to a meeting (in which were included Charles Muses, Reshad Feild and John

Lilly) that, years later, I once heard E.J. humorously refer to as "the Second Council of Nicea." Sheik Reshad Feild, who had just arrived from a centennial anniversary of Rumi in Konya, spoke to us of the fact that the "power houses" were disappearing from Afghanistan and other Eastern Countries and that the center of Work was destined to move to America. In line with this, he would be involved in the setting up of one such "energy center" in Tepoztlán, a place geographically suitable because of the fact of its lying on a ley line. Sometime later I invited Reshad to talk to my older students, and he outlined the project to them. It was necessary to bring together a group of people who had come beyond the need of working on themselves out of a selfish motivation; he was looking for some who were ready to serve, and he hoped that this was the place to find them. Soon after this E.J. offered to select those SAT candidates. Many SAT students came to Crestline and stayed there, not for days, as they had anticipated but for weeks (E.J. most generously fed everybody during this time). Since applying for this selection meant leaving SAT and since only about half remained, (at a time when I was feeling much inclined to withdraw from teaching to regress, regenerate and "put myself in dry-dock"—as I told Charles Tart at the time), I could not fail to perceive E.J. as my benefactor. He did once speak in passing of "taking SAT off my shoulders," so I gave him credit for creating a situation which answered the needs of both my group and myself. The experience of those who arrived in

Crestline, thinking that it was only a selection that they were running into, would take a novelist to describe, and I could not do it since in the course of nearly twenty years the reports I then received have faded too much from my memory. It is my impression that it was a substantial addition to the "work"-education of many, and an adventure—in that some regularities of the ordinary world were suspended. Let me tell, as an instance, how after a certain night of snowing E.J. managed to convince everybody that they were not only snowed in, but (through simulated radio news to the effect that the orientation of the north pole was rapidly changing) created a conviction to the effect that a new glaciation age was upon us. After some time of illusionism those present were convinced that they would never be able to get out of the house and that the best they could do was to prepare for death by lying down on the floor listening to the readings of the *Tibetan Book of the Dead.* And so they did, for days, I was told. (As with all powerful experiences, however, there were some complications: I have made some enemies among those who didn't digest the Crestline Odyssey.)

Ever since, I have known E.J. Gold as a most creative and clairvoyant teacher and friend. It would be too long for a preface to write the story of this acquaintance and I think that I'll rather keep it for an eventual autobiography. Let me just say that during recent years I usually visit him in his Northern California home whenever I pass through the U. S., and every time I return with a happy and grateful feeling—knowing that I received a considerable gift and awed at E.J.'s ability to know something that I needed ahead of myself, who would not have thought of wishing it. Thus, some visits ago, I was introduced by him to the use of a music processor in a computer connected to a synthesizer (so it can write an improvisation). Not long before this I had given up the hope of returning to musical composition— and yet, since then, I have been aiming for a life with room for it in my future. More recently E.J. and the community were engaged in art dealing at an international level, and I received a knowledgeable advice in how to relate with the Chilean government concerning Totila Albert sculptures which I was wanting to restore and preserve.

The impressions described in the foregoing paragraphs will make it clear to the reader of this preface that I'm ready to recommend E.J. to him without needing to read his book. There is nobody that I know that I associate so much with the "devious guide" (*kash mir*) in remembrance of whom (Idries Shah tells us) Kashmir received its name. Also, from his earlier writing I have come to appreciate him as something much rarer than a mere information disseminator: a teacher who *does* something through his communication and stands behind his statements as a presence and a person with whom it is possible to relate.

Claudio Naranjo
Mojacar, Spain
September, 1989

THE SEVEN BODIES

OF MAN

E.J. Gold, *Between Floors,*
oil on masonite, 48" x 60", 1987.

INTRODUCTION

The "I" corresponds to a gradation of Reason. As the gradation of Reason increases, man's corresponding body changes.

The "I" which is the essential self with a partially or fully developed will of presence and attention corresponds to, and can be formally expressed as, a gradation of Reason. There are twenty-one gradations of Reason. Three of these gradations we can never reach as we are or as we can become: the *Absolute,* the *Triplicity*—Metatron, Sandalphon and Shekinah—and *Archangels,* Guardians of the Throne, seated around the throne.

Eighteen gradations of Reason are possible for man or, more exactly, to what he can become.

Man is created in the image of God; as the gradation of Reason increases, his corresponding body changes accordingly, and so, the organic gradation of Reason—or ordinary idiot—has an ordinary body, moving-instinctive, emotional or mental.

There are seven possible bodies of man. More bodies become available to us as the gradation of Reason changes, but the corresponding bodies can no longer be called man; then we are in the category of *entity*. At this point in our evolution, we are not concerned now with very high gradations of Reason.

Each new formation of reason must first pass through disintegration from the old; each new gradation of Reason can be said to be a resurrection, springing from the seed of a former gradation of Reason. Of course, every death and resurrection has its price to pay. The death of each "I" provides the fertilizer for a new resurrection.

The reconciling of all this, that is to say, the blending of the new formation of "I" and the new morphological formation of the body, we call the son. For instance, Son of Man. Son of God cannot be, as far as we know, because son is always higher than parents. \

Unlike most of organic life, in the Real World the son cannot be born while his parents still live. In the Real World, one cannot directly know mother and father, but one can deduce their existence and feel gratitude for their voluntary death.

Voluntary death is a necessity for transformation in the realms of higher gradations of reason.

E.J. Gold, *Just Out for a Morning Stroll,*
oil on canvas, 48" x 60", 1987.

CHAPTER ONE

THE ORGANIC BODY OF MAN

By increasing the repertoire of one's own manifestations one is able to expand beyond one's natural type and form a work type composed of all manifestations possible for false man.

Long ago I gave myself the aim of transmitting all data necessary for formation in the common presences of all interested voyagers a complete understanding of the possible manifestations of the physical body of man and the laws to which these manifestations are subject. Before I begin this task it is necessary for me to clarify certain principles now operating within the sphere of human life on Earth.

It is in the first year of life that we adopt habitually nearly all manifestations we will use for the whole of our lives. Ordinarily only a very few changes in possible manifestation can be introduced after that time.

It is in the first five years of life that specific crystallizations of manifestations are determined; so that after the fifth year of life not even a change in the outward appearance of the manifestation is to be expected. These possible manifestations or as we will call them, postures, are learned in the moving, feeling and thinking centrums and to some degree in the essential self.

When we say that a man is not a Man until he has all possible manifestations of a man, we mean that he has not completed a particular centrum in the early formatory period in terms of all possible manifestations of that particular centrum. He may have chosen only three or four manifestations as necessary to him.

Even if he somehow should form the wish in himself, however contrary to nature, to activate in himself something quite different from his ordinary manifestations, this can occur ordinarily only as a result of mixing two or more of these original manifestations to which he has limited himself.

Later in life if he comes to study hatha yoga, he will be able to form postures only in relation to these same three or four possible physical manifestations. If he studies dance, he will have the same limitations. Even though he may appear to have many manifestations, he will only actually have combinations of these few.

This is why I say that many dancers and actors are in the objective sense bad performers. An actor must have not only many physical manifestations but also emotional postures in his repertoire; he must be able to imitate and not be limited by his ordinary manifestations.

The manifestations of additional emotional postures are impossible for ordinary man. In ancient civilizations there were real actors who could assume any emotional, moving or intellectual posture required to play a role.

Shakespeare, for instance, did not write for real actors. He wrote for actors who could not act. He was forced by circumstance and conditioning to compose in the *bon-ton* literary style of his day.

Because a *bon-ton* actor is able to represent only his own emotional type, he is constrained to express his feelings in the form of dialogue; he is not trained to emanate feelings and silence as were ancient performers. During ancient times, children were encouraged to mimic all manifestations no matter how personally displeasing.

Priests, who taught all possible postures through sacred acting, knew these would be of use in conscious adult life.

In those days a harmonious education meant to teach all possible manifestations of all three centrums, and also, through other means, to demonstrate all possible manifestations of essential self.

Children feel free to imitate others without shame. Because of this they are able to manifest many more postures than adults restricted to their own type. For instance they may learn how to manifest like someone whose manifestations we may feel and think are not at all to be admired or imitated; yet a child must have complete access to all possible manifestations, even those which seem to us to be unbecoming.

One child may not like another's manifestations at all, but the children do not know good from bad. They will imitate anyone who is interesting to them just now.

They do not discriminate between one manifestation and another. All manifestations to them are equally useful in their play. Perhaps later they will discard many of these due to expressions of displeasure or disapproval from those adults and playmates they admire.

In the highly abnormal life of contemporary man, most children are exposed to very few manifestations; thanks to the fears, hatreds and taboos of their elders they almost certainly will not, during the formation of their psyches which takes place largely during the first five years of life, receive impressions of manifestations from all possible types.

In ancient times most families were large and they tended to be much more tribal. Children were subjected to impressions from all members of the community. Everyone in the community was responsible to all children; children were required to come into contact with all members of the community, young and old. Because of this, there automatically formed in them certain predictable impressions and manifesting abilities encompassing the whole range of human life.

A community of work is necessary for children even more than for adults. Adults can learn some new things under special conditions, although their real learning capacity has long since been lost. They can learn to expand possible manifestations of posture, gesture and movement, then increase the number of possible manifestations, then expression, mentation and finally, perhaps, authentic emotion.

Since man, as nature makes him, has no unity and cannot function, impressions must be artificially produced in him at precisely the right moment to crystallize in his appropriate centrum to provide data for work. With real knowledge, it is possible to predict when each of his centrums will become automatically active as a result of suggestion both inner and outer.

Among all those machines here at present, manifestations of all types are represented. If not, we would be forced to provide them. In a school these conditions must now be established artificially because contemporary civilization is unable to provide authentic conditions for life.

Parents today tend to allow in their homes and to play with their children only those whose manifestations conform to their own postures and are more or less the same. Smith does not allow visitors in his home whose manifestations upset him or which he does not understand. This means that many possible manifestations are never seen by Smith's children.

Even in school, there is conformity of manifestations, and in any case by the time children reach school age, it is already too late. The possible education of children in contemporary schools is very limited.

The general manifestations of children in one children's school are very different from manifestations encouraged in another such school. Types never mix fully in those cases.

Perhaps twenty-five manifestations accumulate in the ordinary course of events, for a totality of impressions. Isolated pockets of culture; every type seeks out its own type. Type depends in part upon choice of voluntary and involuntary manifestations.

For instance, if Smith chooses three manifestations in the moving centrum, four in the emotional, three in the intellectual, and two in essence, we say that he is one type, whereas if he chooses quite different manifestations, we say that he is another type. If he chooses only one manifestation out of three possible manifestations for that type, he would still be categorized as that type, even though two manifestations are missing.

To fully master the science of typicality we must have data for each specific category of each type, knowing exactly which manifestations fall into each category. Then one can properly and scientifically divide people into types.

When one knows the type of an individual, then one can predict all his possible manifestations. The aim in this respect is to increase the repertoire of one's own manifestations so that one is able to expand beyond one's natural type, formed accidentally in childhood, forming a work type composed of all manifestations possible for false man.

E.J. Gold, *About to Make the Great Leap*,
oil on canvas board, 20" x 24", 1987.

CHAPTER TWO

THE EMOTIONAL
BODY OF MAN

The battle to master the chronic, the original director of our Emotional Body, is like wrestling with the devil. What was once Heaven for us now becomes a field for a series of voluntary pitched battles.

Data can be transmitted to anyone, but real knowledge only to family, from father to son, across the intervals of isolation ordinarily existing between men of the outer circle of humanity.

Beginning knowledge necessary to enter the Work is called Work Wishing—to wish for something more from life. Voluntary dissatisfaction is the result of many years of immersion in life and the final realization that nothing offered in ordinary life is worth anything in itself.

Work wishing must enter from another octave of influence. This is the first *mi-fa* interval of the school. Here for new candidates there is only one-percent work wish as contrasted to ninety-nine-percent personal wish. Some have at this stage only a whim, others a real necessity.

If the work wish becomes activated, we can make voluntary efforts regularly without outside help, until the *si-doh* interval, at which time another outside shock must be provided in order for us to continue.

The *si-doh* retardation is that period of work on oneself in which one comes face to face with one's chronic—our primary inner entity. During this moment of recognition should the chronic, the machine's own electrically arising sense of personal identity, become aware of our interest, rapid progress past this point becomes absolutely imperative. If one remains passive, the animal will emerge the victor.

Once the chronic is aware of work activities it is only a matter of a very short time before it will begin to struggle without mercy, completely ruthlessly, for its own egoistic continuation.

When the essential self and the chronic come face to face, it is like two adversaries seeing each other for the first time. Along with this shock of recognition there is for both a real smell of danger.

When this occurs, both immediately begin to fight for life. At the most, only three months will pass before we master the animal or it becomes our master.

The chronic can only be mastered if it does not know that it is being mastered. If it becomes aware of these intentional activities it will by all means remove itself from the source of irritation which, in our case, is "the school."

Some schools teach the chronic to overcome the essential self. Pupils of such schools are highly imaginative in explaining to themselves and others the reasons for their self-love.

The introduction of these ideas is sufficient to precipitate struggle. Just hearing these ideas without acting upon them can precipitate real inner disaster.

It is dangerous to arrive at the point-of-recognition when one is not prepared, does not have real techniques, and cannot get help and data for mastering the chronic.

When we wish to activate this struggle, we must summon the chronic with knowledge. To summon with knowledge was originally expressed as *con-jure.*

If we can converse fully with the chronic, we are able to speak with any animal, for all two-brained and one-brained animal languages are the same. This is the real meaning of the story of St. Francis of Assisi who knew how to talk with the animals and to master them with love. It is even possible to do the same with wild animals and even with plants.

To make the chronic obey, we must begin with mastery of the emotional body, the source of ordinary desires. This struggle for organic will begins with the moving centrum. If we know *how to do* in the moving centrum, we have the clues necessary for work in all centrums.

The battle to master the chronic, the original director of our Emotional Body, is like wrestling with a devil. What was once Heaven for us—and which said place we wished formerly to keep as quiet and calm as possible—now becomes a field for a series of voluntary pitched battles. This struggle is a function of Being. It is not something we can decide to do or not to do.

Compare this to the situation of a burglar locked inside a safe accompanied—involuntarily of course—by a bomb set to explode at an unknown time. The bomb cannot be reached and the fuse and timer cannot be dismantled until he opens the safe. He does not know the combination of the safe but has burglar's tools and knowledge of safes and locks.

He must work quickly and effectively. At the same time he must not become upset even once at the possible consequences. While working to release himself he is using up the crucial time he otherwise requires for completion of his urgent self-mission before the uncertain deadline. Perhaps the margin of error is only one moment.

Although the burglar must work under extreme pressure, he must not allow tensions to interfere with his skills. In the same way, we must overcome the chronic and its organic representative, the moving-centrum manifestations of the Emotional Body.

Various factors in organic mastery become important although they were not important before: we must become very cunning. We can exact promises from the chronic in exchange for little things—but these little concessions must be harmless and, if possible, entirely whimsical.

For instance, we can allow the chronic to go to the zoo for one day in return for making a funny face in front of everyone. We must offer something harmless but interesting to the chronic in exchange for something small the machine would not mind performing as a task to pay.

If we cannot think immediately of a way for the chronic to pay, we must not try this idea; only with a definite exchange is this technique genuinely effective. This method is called the *Bargaining Factor*.

After the promise has been extracted, the chronic is given its reward. This is the *Reward Factor*. The chronic should not be totally satisfied, but the reward must not be denied, or it in anger strikes back sometime when our attention is not collected.

To bargain, we must know very well what the chronic wants and what we can harmlessly offer it, representative of *Hu,* or the chronic.

Organic rewards used in making bargains with the chronic are such things as are called *Assisting Factors;* coffee, chocolates, fine French wines. It takes experience to be able to use *Assisting Factors.* We must get the chronic in the organic pleasantly tipsy without getting drunk ourselves.

We must study to find the *Vulnerability Factor* of the chronic in the moving centrum part of the Emotional Body.

In bargaining with the chronic, we must know when we are able to say *no* and when we are not. If we allow the organic self to disobey even once, it will never really obey us again. It will not take us seriously. We must say no only when we have the force to enforce no.

The Emotional Body of Man persists for a while after death. Unlike the Astral Body, it is not capable of separating from the organic.

At funerals, people are more influenced by radiations from the Emotional Body, because during life we put on a *thinking cap*—the formatory centrum—on radiations from the emotional body; they are suppressed, but after death the *thinking cap* is gone and emotional radiations can be sensed more strongly.

The dominant underlying mood during life is expressed as intense emotional radiations.

At my grandmother's death I noticed a particular atmosphere in the vicinity of the corpse, an icy cold feeling, what some people call peace, almost like being in the presence of a vacuum.

Just a hint that an Emotional Body exists should give us the means to impartially observe for hints of its manifestations on the machine and, someday, to get the data to master it by the force of will—the result of *non-identified impartial unity.*

The main distinction between the Emotional Centrum and the Emotional Body is that the emotional centrum is a non-organic concentration. The Emotional Body corresponds with the organic body.

The obvious question is, how can one use the fact that the emotional body lingers on after death?

Ordinarily we expect phenomena only from the perfected Astral and Causal Bodies, but when phenomena were produced in the absence of a perfected Astral or Causal Body I began to become curious about their cause. Investigating the cause of these phenomena, I discovered the Emotional Body of Man.

We can sense the radiations of the Emotional Body. A clue to recognize emotional radiations: they have *resonance;* a particular sensation. The distinction between emanations and radiations: emanations are solar: radiations are planetary. Vampirism is lunar.

Emotional radiations do not vary much; the Emotional Body corresponds with the Organic Body except that it's of a finer matter. There are exchanges of emotional data in the organism, just as we have a quality of radiations we identify as thought.

The practice of necromancy—using a corpse to attempt to make a connection between this world and the world beyond the grave—was used before spiritism became a craze in the late nineteenth century.

Radiations coming from the Emotional Body could become a concern for us if someone in the group died, because of its possible effect on the group vibration. I am reminded of when the great saint died. His followers and even people who hardly knew him were in a state of grief, not good for their work.

Those filing past to look at the body were weeping before they saw him, but in front of the casket there was very little weeping. The radiations emitted from his emotional body canceled most of the effects of the existing personal emotional states.

He often told his followers the essential self could not die. They did not understand what he meant. They thought he was a superman.

When the Astral Body leaves the Organic Body, it does not just fly away somewhere. It *vibrates* in another dimension in which it has always existed and was coated, and now it exists there simply because the probability of its presence in that dimension has increased as the probability of existence in the human sector of the labyrinth has decreased. *It is where it is because it is where it is.*

We can call on cell-memory-data any time we wish—sometimes it is more accessible than others—because cells in the body contain fragments of the organic memory of life on this planet.

One part of the unconscious we could call the conscious part of the collective unconscious.

This is the Being of all entities who have coated higher bodies. They can be contacted from the past or future; time is irrelevant to existence.

How much *entityness* we have developed determines the degree to which this is possible for us.

A small part of us is in everything existing. Our planetary life is under ordinary conditions only an organic concentration. Our organic formation is the source of our arising as an individuum.

Many entities are not individuals—most do not have the organic right-of-existence at any cosmic concentration.

This diffusion of the individual among all organic formations happens only on the planet of our arising. Our ordinary destiny is tied to that planet—or moon—on which we had our arising.

Imagine yourself in many situations accompanied by a corpse. The usual situation of looking into a casket can help, but imagine other situations: riding in a car with a corpse next to you... carrying a corpse—how to get it on the elevator, arm draped over your shoulder walking down the hall, and so forth. Use this idea to arouse the organic *sensation* which invariably accompanies radiations from a corpse.

Now focus on the *sensation* associated with corpses. *If we can discover this sensation we have the Key to the Emotional Body of Man.*

E.J. Gold, *Maternal Warmth,*
oil on canvas, 48" x 60", 1987.

CHAPTER THREE

EMOTIONAL POSTURES

We choose activities out of habit. Some activities we have tried and rejected; some we never knew about and have never been interested in. To try what we have not tried gives us a better chance to choose our path.

By using a "life mask"—a plaster mask cast in a mold made from a person's face—of our own face, and projecting a "death mask" onto it, we can view our faces as they might appear after organic death.

The dominant emotion at death sums up the life, tells the whole story to one who can see—what was accomplished; it provides an objective view of our life. Looking at life from a point of view outside, we can choose a life by viewing the moment of death of the organic body.

The mask can subtly change form, taking on different faces—faces of different nationalities, ages, races—*each expressing a definite whole emotion,* an emotion which, by itself, sums up all the personal experience of a human.

Here is an exercise to try. Hold up your hands in front of you, palms facing the chest, fingertips pointing toward each other. Look at your hands, rippling the fingertips so smoothly and rapidly that they create the effect of living creatures wriggling about. The eerie familiarity of the gesture will probably make you stare in fascination.

Creation occurs All-In-One-Moment. All possibilities are contained in this Great Moment. We exist here, but also in New York, London, and Chicago—these are all different paths we could have taken.

We proceed to a point where the path forks, then must choose branching pathways farther from the starting point, just as a tree branches into smaller and smaller branches. Each of these represents an alternate path we could have taken.

Now slowly put your hands together, fingers interlaced, thumbs lying side by side. This is a *mudra*. Look in the center between the thumbs and see a face. Do not be alarmed. The hands will start melting together. The fingers seem to melt into the backs of the hands and there's a powerful surge of matter flowing down the arms into a waxy lump which has previously been two human hands. Slowly separate the hands because any sudden move might be disastrous. Feel how everything is alive.

We choose activities out of habit. Some activities we have tried and rejected; some we never knew about and have never been interested in. To try what we have not tried gives us a better chance to choose our path.

What does *posture* mean? To explore this we can begin by demonstrating different postures a person might have when death "takes" him. Simulate a voice to go with each posture, such as a man who is ninety-six, sounding old, broken, befuddled, stooped over. This demonstrates that the *length* of life *does not determine its quality.*

With each death posture, we notice the organic posture, facial mask, the whole emotion. We assume emotional postures in addition to the physical.

Some will feel uncomfortable about seeing their own current postures being projected to what they would look like in a few decades, if nothing changed in their Being.

Assume the corpse posture, hands at sides, feet slightly apart. Notice the facial mask corresponding to the organic body posture.

When observing the facial mask, notice a definite skull-like face, with the facial features—eyes, nose and mouth—*obliterated;* just a blank space—nothing at all—a hole in space.

A strong emotion emanates a feeling of expansiveness in the heart; peaceful, tranquil, yet energetic; a feeling of lightness and joy—described as *Love-For-Nothing-In-Particular.* Sit with your back against the wall, legs straight out, feet slightly apart, hands on the floor at your sides. Behind you the walls seem to open up; there is nothing but cold space back there. If there is more than one person, each will feel uniquely alone in the room. Parts of bodies will begin to disappear, but not completely.

Do not try to relax. Increase tension. Make it *voluntary*, then *dis-identify*. See how much force is required to hold tension. We do not resist unless addicted to some special subjective sensation.

Which is phenomena and which is illusion? *All* phenomena is illusion!

Why do you think you are who you are in the organic sense? Do you have the feelings, perceptions and sensations that another one usually has? You only are who you are because you have that machine's habits.

Experiment with subjective views of reality: Look at the feet as two-dimensional drawings, as if one million miles away. With a hand rubbing slowly on the carpet, see as if one million miles distant, as solar systems. This little planet is just one small part of the larger cosmos.

E.J. Gold, *A Soft Job,*
oil on canvas, 48" x 60", 1987.

CHAPTER FOUR

THE USE OF MOOD

In thinking back over moments when we woke up we will notice that each one of these moments is accompanied by a specific mood. Mood is an important key to the emotional body of man.

Some events in life we can remember with such vividness, as if they were happening now, although no apparent reason exists to arouse such powerful memories of these seemingly trivial events.

These are somehow preserved, maybe for eternity, but with no apparent connection to each other or to anything else.

If we think back over these times when we woke up for a few moments, we discover a specific mood which accompanies each.

If we could activate this exact mood right now, this very moment could be preserved in memory just as vividly as it seems to us now in our ordinary walking sleep, because our ordinary impressions are all of past events.

In false man this mood is activated only accidentally, but it is possible, if we have authority over the machine, to activate moods for the preservation of those events and data which are important to our work.

This special mood which can be used to record impressions is an important key to the Emotional Body of Man.

E.J. Gold, *Bebop Man,*
oil on masonite, 48" x 60", 1987.

CHAPTER FIVE

THE MENTAL BODY OF MAN

The mastery of concentrated mentation and attention is indicative of the full development of the mental body.

False man uses ideas to arouse cognitions—a mental form of masturbation—but cognitions are just cream puffs.

We should not at all be concerned about views of the machine and need not concentrate attention on considerings which occur as a by-product of Work—that substance which, following its organic emergence, we call *merde*.

Those who require elaborate and dramatic mental-emotional-cognitions always seem to hold the most artificial imaginary ideas about themselves, especially in relation to the Work.

The first two bodies, organic and emotional, are completed during the process of impartial-observation-of-manifestations-of-the-machine. We can be impartial when we can see the machine *as* a machine —without despair.

During our early work, impartial observation makes change in the Organic Body possible, gaining authority to at least stop the machine from continuing its abuses. Completion of the Emotional Body is possible by impartial observation of the machine just *because we do nothing about the manifestations of the machine.*

We must not observe in the ordinary way— impartiality is the key to inner change.

The Mental Body is developed by concentration-of-attention-to-mentation; that is to say, exact voluntary mentation upon a centrum of gravity question.

Then, having mastered concentrated mentation and attention, we can learn to, just by concentration-of-attention, extinguish a candle flame, even if only momentarily, indicating definitely the full development of the Mental Body.

The so-called magical powers, which can be used as a sacrifice in exchange for a more or less permanent and continuous alarm clock are largely second wind phenomena of a developed Mental Body.

Organic chemical changes can occur through exercises which begin in the imaginary and then, through repetition, become real.

If life depended on your ableness to voluntarily perspire by mental effort alone, could you do it? Use anything; mentation, mood, movement, posture. Use terror, anxiety, visualizing digging a ditch in the hot sun, pushing a car, humiliation.

E.J. Gold, *Haunted Corridor,*
oil on canvas, 48" x 60", 1987.

CHAPTER SIX

REVERBERATIONS

The reverberations of anything we have done extend over many years, and involve many people and results.

Concentrate the full force of attention-of-mentation on something you have done, and then examine mentally all possible reverberations, extending over many years, involving many people, every result, including those events impossible to know in the ordinary way.

Mentally trace all those events which led to your involvement.

E.J. Gold, *Drifting Across the Dimensions,*
oil on canvas, 48" x 60", 1987.

CHAPTER SEVEN

A Day of Presence

The objective recording of a full day of events where we focus on being present should reveal to us some very surprising results.

Here are some examples of the inner monologue we run with ourselves in the course of a typical day of presence which should help to demonstrate the undeveloped Mental Body.

"I...am...here...now...

"In this organic machine...

"The machine, meanwhile, is taking impressions and thinking in response...

"More or less listening and talking according to its associations...

"Considering a general relationship of impressions, associations and sensations as personal emotions, along the lines of conditioned under-standing by now long established.

"But I...who is here now...know better. I know that these are not authentic emotions but sensations grouped together by category...

"Bumbling about and fidgeting in more or less spasmodic response to a combination of outer and inner influences...

"Instinctively sputtering along like an old Model T Ford with more or less the same mechanical dif-ficulties, unless, of course, something else happens to interfere...

"All of which is provided by force from...from...can it be? Can all these manifestations of mine support themselves with just the small quantity of force supplied from three tiny low-volt-age-low-amperage batteries called organic centrums and...and...

"Just where is this endless source of force, the famous sex centrum, when I need it most?

"It only seems to appear at the worst possible times when I am forced to make super efforts...

"My attention is on the whole of myself, I sup-pose, with just enough left over for my outer world which proceeds unaccountably according to the Law of Three whereas my inner world seems unfor-tunately to proceed along the lines of the Law of Seven...

"I know it should be the other way around, but...

"Really, it is as if everything were made of lead...

"This afternoon sometime I must make a more serious effort than I made yesterday to change all this, but at least...at least...I am present, able somehow...perhaps it is just natural to me... to keep a large part of my attention fixed on the idea to remember to be present and at the same time on that windmill over there and those clouds and my appointment later this morning and that round sign and this car just coming up on my left...

*   *   *   *   *   *   *

"Let's see now, I should stop a moment and take stock of my situation, something is wrong, yes definitely wrong, could it be my state?

"No. Then my sensing?

"No. Is my moving centrum on a spree?

"No, it is not that.

"I know I have forgotten something or other, but what?

"Ah yes, not only is all this taking place, but I am part of this picture, the pleasure of my impartial presence is definitely requested. Luckily I have an almost uncanny natural ability to remember to be present while all of this is going on...but wait, but wait!

"What has happened? Here it is the middle of the afternoon and only a moment ago it was morning and...

"I was remembering myself...

"Well, I *was* rather busy...

"I had many things to do...

"First I went to the baker...and then to the bank...or was it the other way around?"

E.J. Gold, *I Thought It Was That Way,*
oil on canvas, 48" x 60", 1987.

CHAPTER EIGHT

THE ASTRAL BODY OF MAN

The completion of the Astral Body of man depends on the accumulation of higher substances which in turn depend on the full and proper functioning of all of our centrums and their assimilation of three kinds of food.

When we speak of completing the Astral Body we must accumulate a new group of substances; these substances must be accumulated differently than ordinary substances.

The metallic salts which coat parts of the Organic Body with the Astral Body are results from *si* 12 of the food octave, aided by the air octave. The air octave is a higher octave which brings lower substances of first food through retardation of the interval by mixture. The blending of higher and lower substances forms a new, slightly higher than the original lower, substance.

Without higher force it cannot rise above the interval. When we are able to combine higher and lower substances the results rise through the interval *as if they were higher substances.*

Although nature supplies us with all the necessary substances to manufacture higher bodies, they are in raw form and unusable for our purposes unless extracted from parental sources and transsubstantiated. It is up to us to make them into useful substances. Nature does not provide this service for us.

We must also learn to collect them in quantity sufficient and direct them to the required places of concentration within our organism which correspond to the cosmic concentrations of all suns and planets. Until we force deposits of these substances, we cannot say we are genuine representations of a higher cosmos.

The work of the factory consists in transforming one kind of substance into another. The organic factory when forced to work for our work receives raw materials and changes them by alchemical means. This process is exactly the same as the ordinary chemical process called electroplating.

Higher substances, which are in fact rare and precious metals, gold in particular, are deposited on certain organic formations. These precipitate and deposit themselves in a coating on the organs necessary to crystallize higher bodies. Electrical force generated by the muscles in certain states and types of effort produces the electrolytic force necessary.

Several factors are necessary. We must learn to extract substances from ordinary sources of matter, then transform them into finer substances which can become metallic salts, alternating with layers of non-conducting substances, sodium, potassium, calcium and manganese in chemical compounds, and finally we must learn to generate sufficient electrolytic force from our muscle systems to support the electrolytic-plating-process.

False man cannot produce electrical energy in his organism; his production of finer substances is almost non-existent; everything is wasted on the operation of the organism itself or expended uselessly as negative emotion, personal pleasures or sensation-satisfactions.

All substances necessary for growth and function of higher bodies can be extracted from three types of ordinary food found in nature: ordinary food, food of air, and mental substances generated in the brain, nervous system and lymphatic gland system when stimulated to arouse specific mental-emotional states.

If we can accumulate a quantity sufficient of finer substances, they can, under the right conditions, precipitate out of solution and deposit in alternate layers of metallic and non-conducting salts over the cardio-pulmonary, vascular, lymphatic and nervous systems, forming higher bodies. The instruction as carried in the *Emerald Tablet of Hermes* tells us to separate the fine from the coarse.

Surpluses of these finer substances can also be used to feed the higher body and provide it with a source for *Hanbledzoin*—higher body blood. Nothing can be wasted on ordinary emotion and mental activity. The physical organism is only able to produce higher body coatings if everything is working properly and economically.

The human organism has the possibility of a very great output of these substances but mechanical man under ordinary conditions of life will never use the factory to its full potential. In mechanical man the factory *is* seldom used for anything. Its elaborate equipment serves a minimum purpose sustaining its own miserable existence.

If we wish to raise the production of the factory to its real potential we would have to learn to save and saturate the whole organism with finer hydrogens. Coating higher bodies cannot be accomplished by any other means.

Growth of higher bodies is a material process just like any other biological-chemical process except that the Astral Body is composed of astral matter and can survive the death of the organic body; the Soul Body is composed of solar matter and is able to exist even after the death of the Astral Body. The Causal Body is composed of matter of the stellar cosmos, substances not belonging to the solar system, and within this solar system cannot be destroyed. In this sense a man who has coated in himself the Causal Body is immortal within the limits of the solar system.

Where can we find the substances necessary to grow these higher bodies? We cannot go far from our planetary sphere, and so we must find them in ordinary substances available to us here on the planetary surface and extract them even though they are not, as a result of several unfortunate cosmic accidents, as easily available on earth as they are on other cosmic concentrations.

The material necessary for the growth of the Astral Body can be found in ordinary food when processed by a healthy organism where blood flow is not restricted by too much muscle tension, and given that the organs of elimination and perspiration glands all work properly. The network of lymphatic glands plays a very important part in all this, and it is these glands which must be coated first, forming what is called the Necklace of Buddha.

When it has formed, the Astral Body will require less of these substances than it did during its initial formation, thus allowing a surplus of substances to be used for the formation of the Soul Body; after this formation has completed itself, the surplus can be used for the formation of the Causal Body, and so on. However, in each case everything depends on the organism as the original immediate source of coarse substances and their transmutation into finer matter usable for these higher being body formations.

Air is a type of food of a slightly higher octave than plant and animal proteins and carbohydrates. By mixing air with ordinary food in a special way, we bring first food substances into this second, slightly higher octave. This occurs in the following way: food first enters the body at *doh,* digesting through *re* and *mi.* It cannot ordinarily proceed past this point unless it is helped from outside.

In order for help to intervene, another outside octave must be introduced. In order to fully process food, to make it a substance for the formation of the higher being body, three different octaves must come into use.

The main octave is the octave of ordinary food, which is to say, proteins, carbohydrates and lipid fats related to transferase functions. To this octave we introduce the octave of air. At the next interval, we introduce the octave of impressions and active thought, which is to say, a deep form of non-seated meditation. These three octaves are thus interconnected.

The *doh* of the air octave is introduced and provides a new note between *mi* and *fa,* a note which we will call X. The *doh* of the impression octave provides the note which we shall call Y, between *si* and *doh.*

Everything man chews and swallows he automatically calls food, but the fact is that from these substances first Being food can be extracted through the use of saliva, hydrochloric acid, and enzymes.

First food is prepared through an organically ordinary mixture of animal and vegetable matter with the assisting substance, *saliva.* Then in the stomach it is prepared further for extraction of first food. Then it goes into the upper intestines, where an important function takes place in extracting 'first food' for use in building the Astral Body.

So what we think of as food is *not* food; it simply *contains* first-Being-food.

We might think that air is Second-Being-Food. But air, too, only *contains* second food which must be *extracted* through *concentration of impartial attention on the whole pulse of the body sensed in the gestalt.*

To extract third-Being-food from impressions—and to add this to our food substances, transsubstantiating them into higher gradations of substance—special voluntary efforts are necessary. Mechanical man does not know how to struggle, nor does he like to struggle. He does not like the sensations which result. To use impressions as a shock, one must create an intentional internal—and totally internalized—struggle. Altogether such techniques, along with a special catalyst, about which entire volumes have been written, make substances available for coating the Astral Body.

He who eats my flesh and drinks my blood has eternal life. To sense the food as the body and blood of Christ and to achieve transsubstantiation of each morsel and drop *before partaking of it,* provides a special energy and attention which can assist in the transformational process.

E.J. Gold, *Sisters in the Skin*,
oil on canvas, 48" x 60", 1987.

CHAPTER NINE

FOOD FOR BEING

The transsubstantiation of food, air and impressions and the extraction from them of essential substances makes them usable in the process of transformation. This knowledge has been used for centuries right in front of our eyes.

Try to sense, concentrating attention on the exact sensations, the passage of these Eucharistic substances through the organic body.

At the same time be receptive to impressions of the emotional vibrations of those who happen to share your table as they eat and process the same sacred substances in themselves.

It is useful to also remember those unfortunate beings who do not presently have the possibility for obtaining food at all.

For now, these impressions will be enough.

The struggle between yes and no must continue much longer. If we obtain an immediate yes or no, a struggle cannot take place. We prefer to end the struggle quickly, to avoid a scene inside our organic selves, so we quickly settle differences with buffers and self-hypnosis.

The head is the centrum of gravity of personality. The moving centrum is the centrum of gravity of the body. The emotional centrum is the centrum of gravity of essence.

The only emotional centrum you know now is what you presently possess; real centrums now are just a dream. Impressions ordinarily pass through perception, then from perception through the emotional centrum. To impressions the emotional attaches the usual subjectives—*like, dislike, good, bad.*

If the emotional is healthy, it can be authentic, just as in a healthy sex centrum, good, bad, like, dislike, pleasure, pain do not attach themselves to sexual feelings. The sex centrum—if it functions correctly—is either *yes,* or *indifferent.*

The function of emotion is not preference and pleasure, but this is how it is ordinarily used.

After going through the emotional centrum, the impression passes to the intellectual memory, and a recording is made along with yes, no, like, dislike... attached by the emotional centrum. A memo is sent at this time to the formatory apparatus, which responds according to its own mood, but the memo must be translated by the formatory and the language of each centrum is different.

The formatory apparatus first types the memo—translating it into her own shorthand—and in *cliché* form passes this on to the moving-instinctive centrum, which translates in a completely different way than formatory intended. As long as this continues, impressions cannot possibly be properly received.

With an all-centrums connection a special common language, the inner language of the Work, is spoken. When first connected the centrums learn the mesoteric language, subordinating themselves to the Work. Then when a genuine connection occurs, they already know how to speak the language of the inner circle and have acclimated themselves to its self-effacing ethic.

By virtue of this, we are automatically initiated as a provisional member of the inner circle of humanity, able to recognize anyone who has attained the same. Not all at once in the beginning, but eventually, we can speak this language with others.

By *trying to attain,* we introduce inadvertently the centrums to one another. By forcing them to work together in this way, we at least get them to stop fighting, if only for a moment or two at a time.

Do not forget that the centrums are in effect business partners. Each of these business partners attends to his own interests, and cares nothing for the interest of the others, only that they fulfill their business functions so that business continues as usual.

The formatory, which is like their secretary, cares nothing at all for the business. Far from helping, the formatory simply uses prearranged shorthand messages. She has a system whereby she is able to use a few prefabricated ideas. She sends *clichés* to save time and memory, so she can polish her nails all day long, or fix her hair.

It is what she wishes to do, and seldom do the bosses pay attention. They do not wish to know what she does. They do not often emerge from their offices, and when they do happen to wander out, they are interested in very different attractions.

In the kitchen and at the dining table more can be learned than anywhere else. If first Being food is not processed, then other activities are useless. Only a cow can chew cud. Other times are more important for other things. Other activities and efforts are also necessary.

If we are not there to do, how can we do? We must not only be *able to do,* we also must *Be.*

Humiliation causes pain. If pain is for you a result of humiliation, then you can know for yourself why this is, and may be able to see this in relation to the octave and in relation to one method used by many monks and nuns for many centuries for the transsubstantiation of food, air and impressions and the extraction from them of essential substances usable in the process of transformation. Penetration beyond this small fragment of a much greater idea depends upon self-initiation, in which one learns to stand on the fragment as a strong foundation upon which leverage can be based toward the penetration of a deeply hidden secret.

At a certain time in one's work, one must go in one of two directions. Work can become personal for the essential self, or for the bigger scale.

But what happens to the remainder of food, after first, second, and third Being foods have been removed?

It becomes *three kinds* of excrementa. Scientists know of only one kind, but there is also a type of excrement from air, and also from impressions, unwanted remainders of these foods.

First-food-excrement is released in an ordinary toilet. The remainder of second-food is released through a special toilet. For this, one must find a very clean toilet. This special excrement can be removed only through sex—not sex for mutual masturbation, but genuine sex to coat the higher body, to obtain data and if possible, to pay for one's own transformation or for the fusion of two or more human shamen into a new formation of multiple being.

The third type of excrement is excreted through speech. Psychologists know of this...exactly nothing.

Substances contained in the air are always present in the atmosphere. Maybe you prefer the air of the Himalayas to the air of sewage. Second food is in all air, first food is in all food no matter what; and then finally there is preference-according-to-type, which dictates the exact form and substance of our three foods.

This relates to another very important idea—the idea of longevity—a most important aim if we are to be of real use to the Work. However, we have no need for longevity for our own amusement and personal survival.

The Emotional Body of man depends on romantic manifestations of the machine and personality. The exact method of building the Fourth Body of Impartial Man—the Astral Body—is *to mercilessly destroy all vestiges of romantic ideas and false manifestations remaining in the machine,* but only after careful impartial and completely scientific empirical observation of the said manifestations for at least two years, sometimes more.

One should never begin this technique without specific and exact guidance. To destroy the romantic manifestations of the machine—or any false manifestations of the machine—can be dangerous and traumatic in the extreme, even when performed under close and competent supervision. In order to destroy all romantic manifestations it is of course first necessary to determine exactly what these romantic manifestations are, and then, as a result of the *impartial* observation of these manifestations, most vanish by themselves. The few remaining romantic manifestations can then be easily eliminated without too much fuss.

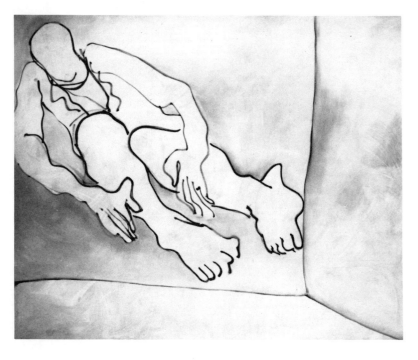

E.J. Gold, *Gathered Up & Ready to Go,*
oil on canvas, 48" x 60", 1987.

CHAPTER TEN

The Soul Body of Man

The complete development for man of the soul can only be accomplished with the crystallization of a fifth body, which alone can be called the Soul Body of Man in the real sense of the word.

Mechanical man has no soul. Only in the course of life is it possible for him to acquire a soul but only through great suffering and special efforts. A soul is a great luxury beyond what is provided by nature and is possible only for a few. For all ordinary manifestations and problems of life, work and procreation, a soul is not necessary.

A soul cannot be born from nothing. It is material as is everything existing, although it is formed of very fine matter. In order to acquire a soul it is first necessary to accumulate the required substance over a rather long period of time.

In order to accumulate the substance required for the formation of the soul we must first know where it originates, of what substances it is formed, and how to accumulate sufficient quantity of these substances.

A soul requires a large amount of special substances; the body only produces a very small quantity each day, which are generally used up in the destructive process of ordinary negative manifestations. We must learn to economize these higher substances and not waste them on such futile organic-emotional trifles.

If crystals are placed in a fixed amount of water at a certain temperature and atmospheric pressure, they dissolve—up to a certain point—after which they precipitate to the bottom of the container. This point at which crystals will no longer dissolve in a solution is called the *point of saturation*. So it is with cell-salts and metals which provide material for the possible formation of the soul.

Continually within the human organism substances usable for the formation of the soul are being produced, but if needed for ordinary manifestations they quickly dissolve and are dispersed to different parts of the body.

There must have been formed a quantity sufficient for crystallization in order to form the soul. The crystallization of these substances takes the same form as the physical body but may be separated from it.

There are many categories of bodies called the soul, but only one of these can be properly called *the* soul. All others are a "soul" only in relation to a lower order of existence.

If we should die before the full crystallization of these substances into a higher body, then along with the death of the organic body the partially formed higher being body also disintegrates, and the parts disperse according to their place of emanation on the cosmic scale.

Parts which originate planetarily return to the planet. Parts which originate in the atmosphere and come from other planets or from the sun return to the atmosphere from which they were taken through the process of extracting second Being food from the air.

Even though the duration of life is different for the Astral Body from that of the Organic Body, it is nevertheless subject to eventual death.

Just like the Organic Body, the Astral Body must live among corresponding conditions and, like a newborn baby, is vulnerable to destruction, starvation, and even—unless it receives a special education corresponding to the world within which it lives—final disintegration.

It cannot exist independently, and just like the Organic Body, if it cannot derive what it needs from the corresponding world in which it exists, it can die.

The Astral Body of man is only a soul when taken in relation to the first body of man, the Organic Body. In this respect it represents the affirming force if we take the Organic Body as the denying principle, with the reconciling principle represented by the special magnetic attraction between them.

This magnetizing force is not possessed by just anyone and without it, mastery of the Organic Body by the Astral is not possible.

The next higher body can be developed only after the Astral Body has been formed.

In relation to the Astral and Organic Bodies, this second higher body can be considered the active principle; the passive represented by the Organic Body, but this time with the Astral Body taking the catalytic part of the reconciling principle.

The complete development for man of the soul can only be accomplished with the crystallization of a fifth body, which alone can truly be called the Soul Body of Man.

Still, this transitional formation is not the *soul* in the real meaning of the word. When the Organic Body dies the Astral Body may disintegrate at the same time, leaving the Soul Body existing by itself. Even though it is immortal in a limited sense, unless it has formed additional higher bodies, it sooner or later will also die.

This Soul Body is immortal within the limits of the solar system and to this body belongs *Real Will,* authority over the machine and an undying devotion to the Absolute and to the Work of the Absolute. It is the master and forms the active principle in relation to all the lower bodies considered as a whole.

Following the death of the Organic Body the first four bodies may become separated and exist apart from one another. It is possible for the Astral

Body to reform itself accidentally within another Organic Body more or less identical with that in which it was formed originally, but the Soul Body is able to voluntarily choose for itself a reformation in the organic world if it wishes to do so.

The devil is the Moon's representative on earth. He considers the substances manufactured in small quantities in the body which can be used for the formation of the soul as his food. He can eat these ordinary seeds every day, but this does not satisfy him, because the seeds are very small.

The devil is therefore willing to give the substance necessary for the formation of a soul because the chances are in his favor that it will not escape his domain.

He can thus choose to sow his seed, taking the chance that it may grow and become larger in quantity and possibly quality. Of course by doing this, he also takes the chance of losing this seed, but as our esteemed Mulla Nassr Eddin said, "Throwing yogurt into the lake may turn the whole lake into yogurt."

Since so few are able to complete this big aim, he loses very little and has much to gain. He hopes that we will eventually exhaust ourselves and drift along in the great river, losing our chance to cross to the other river of evolutionary life.

The battle for souls which occurs between Her Majesty the Moon and His Endlessness the Sun-Absolute does not take place in Heaven, but on planets, because only men, not angels, are possible vessels in which the formation of Real Souls may take place. We are only pawns in this war, but still we have a chance to carve out for ourselves a place in the Work, if we strive against *lunatics,* to become solatics.

Along with the soul must be developed *objective conscience* — not just subjective conscience — in relation to Obligations to the Absolute. Without this additional quality even an immortal soul will eventually be drawn back to the planetary substance and become food for the Moon.

The formation of the Soul Body, the cradle of the soul, or pearl of great price, makes use of substances of ascending octaves, while the formation of the soul borrows from descending octaves to fill the hollow pearl.

E.J. Gold, *Sisters in Spirit,*
oil on canvas, 60" x 90", 1987.

CHAPTER ELEVEN

USE OF THE ROSARY

FORMATION OF THE SOUL

When prayer becomes blended with pulse so that each pulse-beat suggests the sound of the prayer being repeated, we are ready to use this as an irritant for the formation of a pearl—the Soul Body.

The word *bead* originally meant *incantation*, to do *holy bidding*, to perform the sacred obligation, the repetition of prayers.

When it was necessary to keep secret the sacred incantations, prayers were represented as knots, and later, by beads.

What is the use of the prayer bead system? What is their technical use? How is prayer extracted from the rosary, from the prayer beads? How do the beads, unconscious, repetitive, become prayer so powerful we can throw the beads away?

Beads are, in themselves, empty artifacts. In the beginning a prayer is imposed upon them. Not everyone is given the same prayer to be used with beads; like a prescription, one does not take drugs prescribed for someone else. Although it is the same spoon, a different medicine fills the spoon.

Mantra, zhikr, movements, remembering exercises, aphorisms, koans, counting exercises, rhythmics, are all related to prayer beads in a very special way.

It is not whether a new thing can be found but whether an old thing will serve. The key question is economy. We may dream of a new or better method, but if we have a method which works, why not use it? We should use the method we know; only then will we be qualified to search for a new method.

Placing prayer in beads is relatively easy; *extracting* prayer from beads takes longer; we are freeing ourselves from one set of bonds sufficiently to begin work on a more subtle set of bonds, and the beads are the first and most visible outer form of the technique. In the beginning we must have a goal to someday extract from the beads what we have put into them—to take back what is our own. This idea is very significant in relation to our presence here on earth. We must not forget that someday we intend to take back what is our own.

Use of beads without extracting what one puts into them is less than one tenth of the method. Anyone can use beads, but not everyone can learn to extract from the beads the prayer that was placed in them.

Pulse is the resisting force; the heart pumps the blood; the pulse answers.

A heartbeat is localized; the pulse more generalized, spread through the body; it is more useable for work because we can sense the pulse as a whole; we can be particularly sensitive to it when we assume the posture represented by the crucifixion.

As we can see, real prayer is not a primarily mental idea; it is based on repetition and pulse. Ultimately we intend to extract prayer from an artifact—not just any prayer but a prayer which was given to us as a specific remedy, a *prescription*.

In some traditions the idea of listening to one's heart has been preserved, but until we organically fill it with prayer, the heart has nothing to say.

Prayer of the heart reverberates automatically with the pulse, and becomes an irritant to make what has been called the Pearl of Great Price. Prayer carried by pulse is the exact irritant, and higher bodies can form around this irritant. If performed incorrectly, the heartbeat prayer stops and so does everything else.

We can begin this work with the idea that we came from somewhere else, and landed like an airplane in a human biological machine. However, arising as an individuum can now occur for the first time in this human form we inhabit. There are undoubtedly parts which have existed since the beginning of time—cell colonies... spiritualized parts also, which are not complete.

There are influences which act upon us which are not genuine parts of ourselves, but which seem to be natural to our existence because we are taught—and most of us come to believe—that they are.

Our arising and formation in the organic world are all we have to work from in our efforts to induce the formation of higher bodies. If we treat this life as our one opportunity to make a change, then we can understand better how to work with what we really have and not with what we imagine ourselves to have. We really cannot afford to waste time throwing away our supernatural resources and giving to organic life what it asks from us.

We must know how to organize our time and efforts with economy. We cannot afford to squander our time on daily existence. We must do some things every day toward our daily existence; we cannot afford to turn our backs on organic life, yet we cannot devote all our time to it. We must find a way to work which allows us to give some time and attention to organic life and at the same time do our higher work.

At some point it will also be necessary for us to learn how to do the Work with economy of emotion and for this purpose the "pulse-prayer" is well-suited.

The method of transference to the pulse of a prayer specific to each individual can be of use to us because it is a beginning method which allows us to work both for the higher and for ourselves. But before the prayer can be placed, the body must be prepared.

The heartbeat and respiration may be *indirectly* altered through the use of the moving centrum, not haphazardly, but in definite ways specific for each individual. The machine must be repaired, prepared, then loaded and charged with the prayer.

When the prayer becomes merged with the pulse only then can we dispense with the string of prayer beads. There is no reason for us to use them for the rest of our lives. When the prayer becomes blended with the pulse, so much so that each pulse-beat automatically suggests the sound of the prayer being repeated, we are ready to use this as an irritant for the formation of a very special pearl—the Soul Body.

The prayer for beads is given to each individual only after a long period of observation because a real heart-prayer becomes a parasite, firmly bonding the essential self to our pulse for a while.

If properly used, the heart-prayer can not be extracted from the pulse until the death of the body. We do not use a mantra or zhikr given as a prescription to another. This explains why there is secrecy in these matters. We do not give away or lend our prayer to others.

Has a song ever repeated itself mentally, no matter what you do, refusing to stop? For longer than a day?

We cannot exorcise such a song; it only stops when it has somehow exhausted itself or been replaced automatically by some other fixation through the thought process of association. Imagine a tune so powerful it does not die for the rest of your life; if we begin on this path, we must make sure it is the correct and effective remedy leading to a truly higher formation of a soul.

"Let God kill him who teaches and does not know"; one must not give prayer or zhikr unless one knows exactly which prayer to give.

It's like learning to swim by just dipping your big toe in the water; until it is too late we do not know if a prayer will work. If we really try, a prayer becomes part of our pulse, then begins to do its work.

Diagnosis and remedial results are very slow, requiring trial and error. A different repair method is indicated for each typicality.

For a "type three" a "number seven prayer" is given to get the result "ten". We do not add seven to two or seven to nine. Each prayer represents a number when we want the result to be ten. Each typicality corresponds to a prayer on the other end of the stick.

When the heart begins to reverberate with prayer, it sends roots to the nervous system and blood; the machine vibrates with the sound of the prayer, reinforced by habitual repetition.

We can train our ears, after a long time, to hear what seem to be angelic vocal reverberations, evoking in ourselves words, which, after many thousands of repetitions in time to the pulse, the throbbing of the whole body, seem to be our own prayer.

Lie down and as you do so, notice the throbbing of the whole body. The heart beats, the body answers with pulse and the bloodstream has its own pressure. The shock of entry of blood from the exhaling valve of the heart echoes through the whole arterial system. Of course, the nervous system is also directly affected by this. The nervous system initiates and monitors the pulse and tells the heart to pump faster or slower.

We can consider the Organic Body merely as a container, a device which exists solely for the purpose of originating and reverberating the heart-prayer; however, if we depend on just the Organic Body, when the Organic Body ceases, our prayer will stop. This little thought should function for us as an irritant which forces us to discover exactly how to use the human biological machine as a chemical factory and to function in a very different way.

Prayer, when vibrated with the organic circulatory system, is one of the larger uses of sensing. If we cannot sense pulse, we cannot use pulse for automatic prayer. Ordinarily to continually sense the pulse would be annoying. Eventually, extremely aware of pulse, we can use the throbbing of the body to suggest prayer; we are suggestible so we should, if we are cunning, use our ordinary destructive self-suggestion for our work on self, and in this way, we can use our weaknesses as strengths—*Jiu-Jitsu Yoga;* if we are suggestible, we should use self-suggestion. If we are influenced, we should put ourselves under influence. If we are forgetful, we should use our forgetfulness to help us remember attention of presence. If we are lazy, we should use our laziness to arouse ourselves from inertness.

However, we are a little ahead of ourselves. First, we must observe ourselves under work conditions for a long time to be sure. We cannot afford to make a permanent mistake.

In addition, the machine needs a certain amount of preparation.

E.J. Gold, *Enwraptured,*
oil on canvas, 48" x 60", 1987.

CHAPTER TWELVE

THE PRAYER WHEEL

For the heart-prayer to be effective, we must be able to actually hear and feel the sound-reverberation of our prayer in the throbbing of our pulse.

The use of the heart-prayer is to transform the whole body into a soft perpetual Prayer Wheel attuning itself to the pulse of all living things until everything suggests the sound of our prayer.

The body becomes an organic prayer drone. The drone can be sustained collectively, but then requires a choirmaster. Esoteric orders find this easier than public church congregations.

In reference to the real use of prayer beads, Church recitation has a definite hypnotic effect. But the exercise is of real use only individually and privately.

For those who have not learned prayer as children it is necessary in the beginning to repeat the prayer aloud until the sound reverberates mentally with the same force as verbal repetition.

We must be able to hear the sound-reverberation of our prayer in the throbbing of our pulse and, moreover, as the distinct unique sound of our own voice.

E.J. Gold, *Really Reaching for It,*
oil on canvas board, 20" x 24", 1987.

CHAPTER THIRTEEN

The Causal Body of Man

The great finesse is to withdraw at the moment of greatest possible identification when we have reached our peak of advancement, or social success, or whatever it is that we have strived for in an ordinary way.

Those who are of the Work cannot be successful in the ordinary mechanical way, although in the sense of Work success is possible and even, in some cases, unavoidable. Those who are really in the Work do not require the approbation of monkeys. The inner-circle recognizes success in the sense of an accomplishment, *to make something.*

Romantic and passionate situations offer a greater chance for identification, to draw us into a state in which we could easily remain.

The great *finesse* is to withdraw at the moment of greatest possible identification; home, children, love, business. For example, we reach the position of chief executive of a company and at the same moment withdraw, when we have reached our peak of advancement, the point of greatest possible identification.

Another example would be to build a fortune at the craps table and then say "I pass." It would not be correct to—on the highway—suddenly turn around and climb into the back seat; this is not *finesse,* this is *stupidity.*

Timing, *finesse,* and exactitude are all qualities which belong to a man of the Work. For example, I happen to need money for my work. I see someone who can help me who is very wealthy and, moreover, well disposed to me and my work...Let us say, an easily manipulated *bon-ton* dowager.

She is thoroughly enamoured and, to gain attention, would do almost anything. I invite her to sit with me at my restaurant table; carefully I nurture her affection until at last she is ready to sign a check for any amount.

Then, just as she reaches for her pocketbook, I allow saliva to dribble from my half-open mouth onto the front of her silk blouse, at the same time expostulating vividly on the finer techniques of objective defecation in the Persian style, graphically demonstrating by use of moving-centrum-postures, each point in e-l-a-b-o-r-a-t-e detail...At which point, her hand suddenly stops its downward motion toward the purse. This is what is really meant by sacred gymnastics, a game which higher entities play—their sole purpose for involvement with organic life.

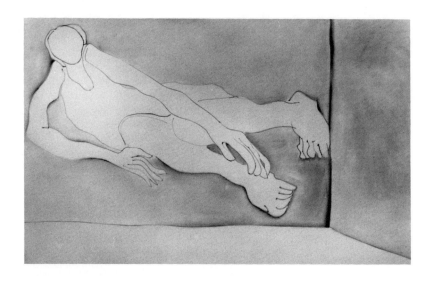

E.J. Gold, *Symposium,*
oil on canvas, 60" x 96", 1987.

CHAPTER FOURTEEN

THE ANGELIC BODY OF MAN

Every meal could be a Last Supper, not only in the sense of transsubstantiation of substances, but also in the personal sense.

If we have a number of people in a room, their combined breath makes a certain atmosphere, plus the smell of food and the smell of the spices; the use of certain spices on certain days for certain people; the type of lighting effect—windows open or closed, for example; certain behavior directed or choreographed by the toastmaster; feelings of the group for each other—good, bad or indifferent; moving centrum activities; how quickly or slowly the food is served, plates cleared; sometimes even the seating arrangement can be crucial in the esoteric sense of the word.

Then the clearing of the table, putting away of the invoking force, food and air mixed with impressions as with saliva; special readings can supply not only impressions and psychoemotional thought-forms, but also an active psychological state useful and indispensible for the transformation of substances. Every meal could be a Last Supper, not only in the sense of transsubstantiation of substances, but also in the personal sense.

There are specific postures for every type. It is possible to match manifestations, tone, gesture, even to speak simultaneously in the exact tone, anticipating the next manifestation even before the person himself or herself sees it coming.

Americans like the sound of grief. Russians like drama; English, resignation; French, expostulation and Irish, brawling. But Americans dearly love their sadness. If the Irish wail, then Americans incessantly bitch, gripe and groan.

E.J. Gold, *In Repose,*
oil on canvas, 60" x 96", 1987.

CHAPTER FIFTEEN

GRADATION OF REASON

Organic shame can be used to form a wish for the essential self. If we know we are not real man, we can wish to be.

Who works on self races against a time-bomb which may explode at any moment. Even so, he must be professional, having a sense of urgency blended with competence.

Very few who hear of Work ideas wish for authentic data and even fewer wish to *do*. This keeps most men in a very real and inescapable prison with no doors.

As we can see man with our inner eye, he is a machine under many influences beyond his knowing or control. To wish to be no longer subject to the biological laws of accident is a good beginning work-wish.

Early observation of the machine provides good data for organic shame; organic shame can be used to form a wish for the essential self. If we know we are not real man, we can wish to *be*.

Identification is *non-presence,* while one who is not able to vibrate "I" and "Here" to make the third-force-being is a *nonentity.*

If we could see ourselves in five dimensions our bodies-in-extension would look to us like spiralling worms. In this body we could view past and future as a single event. Our three space and one linear time dimension bodies are cross-sections of a much larger whole.

Another way of looking at this is as a tree of destiny, with all the possible courses of our destiny branching out at each intersection. This is also called the thousand-headed cobra, upon whose coils Krishna and Radha sit... however, Krishna and Radha are actually part of the serpent.

Another way of looking at this is that all suns are in reality connected as an emotional body of the Absolute, but as they intersect three dimensions and are viewed only occasionally in four dimensions by man, they appear to be separate solar bodies.

In six dimensions, we look even worse-than-worms. It is best to not sit on this stool too long because not only can little be accomplished in this state, but it is in addition not a very pleasant experience.

The All-Suns body is ordinarily viewed in only three dimensions, and so it appears much the same as fingers would appear to beings living in a piece of paper. Although they are part of the same hand—and when viewed as a whole are completely different in form and function—as they intersect the plane of the paper they seem to be circles which grow and shrink in size and are entirely unconnected. From the point of view of the paper, they seem to have no use in the cosmos.

In the same way, we view the body of All-Suns like the blind men examining the elephant. Man knows his universe only from this same viewpoint.

When three or more centrums are connected and coated, forming a higher or slightly higher body than that organic hodge-podge known as man, we can no longer use the term *common-presence* to describe *presence-taken-altogether*. To be more exact, we must use the term *gradation of Reason*.

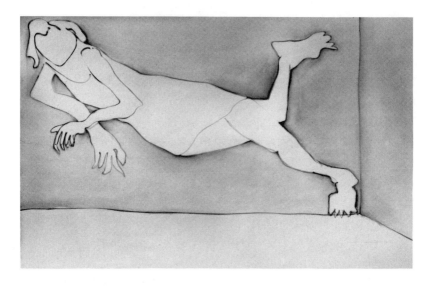

E.J. Gold, *A Wee Slip of a Girl,*
oil on canvas, 60" x 96", 1987.

CHAPTER SIXTEEN

INVOCATIONAL DINNERS

No one ought to be given a premature ticket to the next world. This is one of the dangers of accepting guests to our invocational dinners, but this should not be a problem if instructions are followed exactly.

The formal dinner is modeled after the Last Supper. Through the action of the substances in the food a special force is transmitted which slowly may transform those present at the table in the work circle.

The setting and arrangement of the table has its corresponding in the angelic world, and the dinners served provide the necessary lower substances for the evolutionary conditions referred to in the law, 'As Below, So Above.'

What produces the functioning force of a working circle sitting in such a seance? The electromagnetic force can descend through the presence of the angel who is attracted by the correspondence of the work circle's invocational dinner chamber with the corresponding angelic chamber under the law 'Like Attracts Like', the visible effects of which can be seen in the process of ordinary life just by observation of courting couples out for a Sunday stroll.

On those in the work circle the effect of the invoked presence is transformational; but it is very gentle and over a long period of time. It requires many repetitions of these invocational dinners which produce a continual irritation of the soul and which force evolution in self-defense. Evolution does not occur by our efforts to evolve; evolution occurs as a result of putting ourselves into a situation in which we are forced to evolve.

In what other way can we provoke evolution? We can also, at the same time, add another factor to the scene of our struggle to force our evolution. Through the habit of attending these invocational dinners, the habitual expectation itself of the assembly of the work circle can perpetuate by momentum after organic life. In this case through performing the ritual invocational dinners, we can sense the force of the ritual. Developing the momentum of these work habits is really the meaning and the force of all rituals. The point is, if we accustom ourselves to expect to attend an assembly such as this invocational dinner, we will be able to assemble later, due to the momentum of our habit, with some vehicle which is higher than our organic body.

There is an additional factor which will become of interest to us when we examine it a second time. The association of special food and congenial company with the ideas has the effect of producing two results.

The two results of which we speak are, first, the association of the special food, which is made during the dinner, the congenial company, and the atmosphere of warmth, with the ideas. The congenial company and the atmosphere of warmth at the same time are important for the second result, the natural production of an exact mood, a necessary component for the invocations which is furthermore complemented by the invocational reading.

In addition, at these invocational dinners there is the alchemical blending of the typicalities as represented by the guests present which forms the automatic production of a series of alchemical solar substances through the organism, for activating the higher centrums. Once the centrums wake up and remain awake, they can continue their evolution without the organic...voluntarily.

The community as a work circle includes different typicalities, and for the production of the conditions for their work toward evolution they must endure the company of each other in the study circle. Everyone who is attracted to a study circle is not of the same typicality. If everyone were of the same typicality, although this may create a more comfortable social situation, the circle would not function properly because a circle composed of only one type would not invoke.

We can understand this if we examine a radio. If all the parts are the same, the radio does not function. It is obvious. But when all the components of the radio are assembled with exactitude the radio functions as a whole greater than the sum of its individual parts. In the same fashion, the study circle as a functioning whole composed of all the typicalities composes something greater than the sum of all the typicalities themselves. Certainly, this is what we need.

If we think of evolution as resulting from exposure to angelic evolving radiation, of an invoked presence, we must realize that it is necessary to expose ourselves to the radiation and at the same time to expose ourselves only a little at a time. Too much angelic radiation is not good for the health.

If we know how to cook well, we can put evolutionary substances in the food we serve at our table. At the invocational dinner the substances of food are transformed by the invoked presences of those who prepared it, and those who partake of it, and through our impressions of the mood and atmosphere created, and impressions of the reading as it is read aloud, which when taken altogether provide all which is necessary for the automatic and semi-voluntary needs of the presences of the various typicalities.

At the same time, it is not necessary to depend only on the food prepared and the company assembled to produce an invocation. Although the alchemical blending of these impressions are necessary, there are other invisible factors, hidden from the ordinary vision, operating on the group.

Even without the exact formation corresponding to the angelic presence and radiation we wish to invoke, if we have the courage to pay attention to the mood and the force present at these dinners, we are then able to study the dynamics of invocation. For this, we use the circle. The circle is the basis for the choreography of the invocational dinner.

We do not wish to invoke involuntarily because this may produce the descent of undesirable entities. We must not fall into the game of the medium, the clairvoyant and the psychic. They invoke, but they do not know what exactly they invoke. We must invoke with exact knowledge. The knowledge is from long experience of thousands of years of practical efforts of those who have come before us, and of those who came before them, and of those who came before them....

Then our discussion must pass to the question of voluntary activity and also work associated with the community, because it is the activity of the whole day which constitutes the invocation. In a community of work the question of all the other activities of the day centers around the table. The kitchen serves the community by producing special food from which we must extract substances for our work; because of this, the kitchen is called the heart of the community.

In the evenings when we invoke, we must realize that all our attentions since the morning form the parts of the invocation. The total invocation includes all the voluntary and involuntary activities of the day. If we could voluntarize all these activities they could yield something desirable for our evolutionary invocations and for our preparatory work cultivating ourselves as receptive fields for this evolutionary force.

The question of involuntary activities has great importance in regard to everything we are making efforts towards in the struggle of voluntary evolution.

Who is invoked by the voluntarizing of our typical involuntary activities? This is a question if we do not know ourselves well enough. We concentrate attention on the significance of data given during the invocation of presences, but we should be more concerned with the question of exactly how our involuntary activities affect the evening invocation.

The activities during the day affect our invocational dinners; in fact these activities, if voluntarily performed, produce the fundamental necessity essential for an invocation in the work circle each evening. Because we do not have empirical data to know what our typical activities invoke, to effect an invocation we must rely on the form of the invocation. The form *is* the content. This is a basic law of invocation.

However, in order to use empirical data about our daily activities and how they affect our invocational work, we must know how to examine the objective activity of the machine. This examination of the machine's activities is like watching a grand ballet. It is our lineage of work.

In fact we are trying to observe the *Ballet of the Sorcerers*—the involuntary sorcerer representing those fractions of small 'I's' of the machine which stubbornly defend various petty concerns which are held by the machine at different times. By intentionally setting one conflicting fraction against another simultaneously, we provoke a struggle for authority over the machine, producing results which add to our efforts to produce the force necessary for the transformation of substances for our work. Yet, to produce this ballet, we must be able to remain impartial in the observation of the machine, and we must have objective knowledge of the activities of the machine, disregarding their subjective socio-emotional significance.

So we may be able to, after much time spent on the practical study of this question, determine the function of our daily machine activities—those involuntary activities the functioning of which indicates that we are manifesting according to ordinary, mechanical laws of the machine as distinct from the functioning of the voluntary activities—in regard to the fact that both form a part of the invocation. But for the practical study of this question, observation of the very obscure aspects of one's typicality—the ordinary, involuntary activities, those activities we consider most trivial—is necessary. Those involuntary activities we believe most insignificant are usually the barriers to real work.

At the same time, voluntarizing these activities is like intentionally developing any muscle. We tend to exercise certain muscles which are the most developed, but may resist the opportunity to exercise uncustomary muscles. The muscles which are undeveloped can produce pain when we insist on their obedience.

Just as in a chemical reaction in which a catalyst activates the process of combining individual components to form a new substance, there is a corresponding catalyst for the evening assembly of a community of work. This catalyst is the invocational dinner, for which there is also a catalyst; and for the reading and the discourse, and for the preparations of all the arrangements for the evening, other catalysts—shocks—are necessary for their activation.

In the preparation for a seance we must assemble a group of people representing all the different typicalities of organic presences which we can locate and attract to our study circle. Then if we wish to have a functioning study circle, we must learn to tolerate the presences of other typicalities as they are, not as we would prefer them to be for our accommodation.

We can determine the typicality present through the scent, the fragrance, or the odor we detect if we have developed and trained our sense of smell. It is a delicate fragrance in the case of our own and similar typicalities, but in the case of very different typicalities, the odor is more like a stubborn and offensive fart.

However, even the emotional and mental emanations of our own typicalities assembled in a group can be difficult to tolerate, and unless we can voluntarize our emotions to remain organically impartial toward the involuntary emotional manifestations of others, the invocation cannot succeed as we wish. The emotional emanations of other typicalities in the group may be very difficult to endure, yet this is one small price we must pay to be able to work.

We also in an assembled group hear the results of the presence of the involuntary mental emanations springing from the intellects of other typicalities. Therefore, we must learn to remain impartial toward these intellectual 'atmospheres' involuntarily produced because we do not have sufficient knowledge concerning the general atmosphere necessary for the invocation for which purpose the work-circle has gathered.

In addition, as in all chemical reactions in which different elements are combined to form a compound that, by definition, is characterized by entirely new properties than formerly possessed by the previous distinct elements, the corresponding process can be observed about the chemistry of the different typicalities of a functioning work-circle. Just as in a chemical reaction, we must expect these different typicalities to blend and function as a working work-circle which may invoke a presence recognizable by entirely new qualities. During an invocation, the presences of the individual personal typicalities ought to become psycho-emotionally and also organically invisible as the resultant blending occurs for the descent of an invoked presence upon the circle. We set the stage for the function of this blending process as we sit in this circle and partake of dinner together.

To make evolution possible requires the work-circle, along with the active catalyst chemistry of the food, blended and acted upon by the atmospheres produced by the different typicalities composing the circle, to attract an invoked presence to descend. Through invocation, the passage of a presence will cause the production of alchemical by-products within the chemistry of the participants sitting in the circle.

The mere passage of the presence of an angel effects an alchemical transformation. It is an internal transformation, and the productive results are cellular salts or noble metals and rare earths which are deposited through the lymphatic system, eventually forming what is known as the Necklace of Buddha.

Everyone has a lymphatic system, but we must find something in the chemistry of our typicality which can cause the lymphatic system to become for us the grain of sand which will provoke an exact irritation as in an oyster—an irritation which can be coated. This coating of the lymphatic system forms the fourth, Astral Body which is the transition body to the Soul Body, and, at the same time, causes a further irritation which can be coated, like the formation of a pearl, which through further balanced development could become the Soul Body. The greater the irritation, the greater the pearl. It is necessary to coat the irritation or die.

In other words, the lymphatic system must be exposed, so it can be struck by lightning. This gives us the possibility to evolve because the formation of higher bodies enables one to acquire a special non-organic longevity. On the other hand, there is also a very big corresponding risk.

That active principle which produces voluntary evolution is called *Prayer Absolute.* Man and angels were created with the original function not as 'messengers,' but as *conductors,* to attract and invoke upon themselves the lightning, the ordinarily static electricity, of the Absolute. During this process if one does not change, one will be annihilated in the worst way, that is for sure.

But the electrical force of the Absolute could be retarded, allowing one to gain more time to work for the possibility of becoming a lightning rod for the Absolute, achieving as a result both transformation and evolution. And gaining time to become a voluntary part of this process, one can thereby retard the inevitable destruction to the nervous system for a very long time.

As one of these conductors, the first destroyed would be the organic and, if one has not worked on oneself, nothing will remain. But for man who has worked on himself in the course of working for the Absolute, being destroyed in the organic is just an occupational hazard. Prayer Absolute is obviously a shock, and if we choose to pursue this method of evolution, we must work quickly with constant attention on our aim, to form higher bodies while we still have the organic body in which to make the necessary efforts.

What part does the invocant play in voluntary evolution? Is the invocant the evolution process itself?

With the proper conditions and exact direction, only then can the conditions of work produce evolution. It is easy to see that we have much to do. First it is necessary to acquire all the background data possible and to learn to voluntarize the machine's daily activities.

There are some in the circle who make it function more weakly, but even so, we can be aware of presences if we are aware of our subtle sensing.

The study circle, without experience, by strictly following the instruction, could produce an invocation but be unaware of results. Of course, there is a risk. If the day had been very involuntary for members of the circle, or contaminations were acquired by carelessness and inattention, it could go badly. The odds of that happening depend on the events of the day.

This is not an ordinary seance nor an ordinary dinner. In addition to the small evolutionary change, a possibility opens the door to other things perhaps invisible....

What food is to the satisfaction of ordinary desires, the circle is to the satisfaction of higher desires. But the satisfaction of ordinary desires is the first problem.

Most people believe they understand the idea of the necessity to satisfy ordinary desires and cravings. However, what do you think is the most powerful of biological addictions? It is not sex as you may expect. It is food. It is not even filling your belly. It is simply 'stuffing your mouth' which forms and determines the thought and conversation of biological-mechanical man.

You invite people to attend a dinner. Then present these ideas in your discourse. If an invocation takes place, there will be perhaps people who leave and do not return, in which case they have no need of these ideas in spite of their initially-formed interest.

Few have the equipment to understand, and of those, even fewer have the discipline for this work. And of those, even fewer come to the Work.

Then the question arises, do we know whom to invite as guests? Who will come to our table? You would not wish to invite everyone to your house, in which case, sample those people interested in these ideas, by first serving these ideas in a public cafe. We will sow seeds, taking the risk that they fall on barren soil. In other words, serve these ideas as food, to poison people against biological life, and perhaps dispose them toward the Work.

But perhaps you would prefer to invite guests to your house? Perhaps after three or four months you will have a group so cohesive that you will wish to have the dinners at your own home.

When we set the table for dinner we leave one place unoccupied in addition to the number of invited guests, for a guest who may seemingly by chance come to our door.

We will have ordinary company and also important people may come to our table. Since we cannot judge the significance of the importance of the guests, we must not presume to judge. One cannot make a judgment by the manifestations, certainly, nor by the appearance of a guest.

The manifestations and the appearances will be deceptive. If one is truly exalted, he may seem to be the lowest according to appearances. It is a common ruse. And if one seems exalted through one's manifestations, often he is base.

But in the real world, everyone is exalted, everyone is at the same place. Sometimes some of them disguise themselves.

How do we know the difference between those who are serious and those who come to our table just to taste and to nibble at the food like dilettantes? If their attention is on the Work, or if it could be attracted in the future to the Work, they should be at these dinners. Then they will unconsciously associate the ideas with a special and a natural activity.

Even if they just taste the food and dimly remember the ideas, they will always have a good association for the Work. Even if they do not have this, and cannot construct a relationship between the ideas and the food, they will have an attachment of emotional significance with the experience provided by attending the invocational dinner.

In examining this method of presenting these ideas, there are two streams of thought, but only one idea. It is important to understand the idea of a study circle and how it is possible for individuals who have never been in a group working with the ideas to start a study circle. This is insisted on. The awareness must someday dawn on us that work as a member of a circle of invocation is necessary at least for a certain time.

We will also attract people "with many zeros" to our dinners and perhaps they may also hear the ideas through the barrier of money. People are attracted to the meals through an invisible magnetism, like to a net which traps fish. We may accidentally trap the big fish with the little fish, and also the fish who know how to eat but do not know exactly what it is they eat.

Why use the sacred invocational dinner to attract people to these ideas? Because people only respond to their bellies and the dinner is the bait. When the fishes are caught, then we sauté them and serve them on our table to create a special atmosphere.

How do we know that we have attracted all the different typicalities necessary for the circle to function and for the invocation to produce voluntary evolution in self-defense? Most groups collect all similar typicalities, in which case either they do not invoke or they invoke the same limited presences again and again.

Hosting these dinners requires ample sums of money to purchase the food for the meals and to furnish the setting of the table and the atmosphere of the chamber with all that is necessary to create the proper conditions and the appropriate mood.

Now we will address the question of how, exactly, to organize the circle. Each time we encounter a prospective guest, we are given very exact instructions as to how to choreograph the meeting and how to lure our potential guest to dinner. We leave nothing to the imagination or to chance in the exact process of forming a study circle.

For instance when first meeting someone who expresses an interest in these ideas, rather than discussing the Work ideas we may choose to give them a business card which we have had printed. Even the business card is very exact and according to a format specifically designed for the purpose of captivating the attention only of someone seriously intrigued by these ideas.

Then if they are interested in attending a special gathering with the aim of penetrating these ideas, we instruct them to contact us on a specific date and at a specific time which we notate on the card we have given, being very careful to select a time when you are certain to be available. Further, you can assign them a date and time according to your personal code which will remind you where and when you first encountered the caller and even the details of the situation. For example, people you meet on Mondays at a certain restaurant will always be told to call on a Monday six weeks from that date at three o'clock in the afternoon.

If the people we meet have sufficient attention, over an extended period of time, rooted on their search for these ideas with the serious aim of penetrating to real knowledge, this can be determined to some degree by the fact that they remember to contact you as suggested to obtain more information about these special meetings. And perhaps they will have been able to taste something during this first encounter which attracts them to the circle of invocation.

Then, only offer an invitation to *one* such special meeting which, fortunately for them, has been arranged for this same particular evening. Thus they have very little time to take an active step and to arrange their affairs in order that they can attend the meeting and pursue their expressed interest which may be or may not be, as yet, gnawing at their attention. On the other hand, if this meeting is not important enough to confirm the invitation, then they should not be given another opportunity unless they are unable to come because they are bound by a commitment falling under the category of something serious.

The protocol of sacred invocational dinners is exact. Each invitation to a prospective candidate demands immediate attention. The purpose of the invitation is to qualify the interest, sincerity and the attention span of a prospective candidate.

The invitation is presented like a key to open the door into the invocational chamber, which may or may not be obvious to guests who have arrived simply to share a warm, congenial evening meal.

But there is a risk. When accepting hospitality as a guest one must have authority over one's manifestations just as an animal must be housebroken to remain in the house. On the other hand as host, we are also responsible for the presence of our guests whom we have invited to sit with us at our table.

No one ought to be given a premature ticket to the next world. This is one of the dangers of accepting guests to our invocational dinners, but this should not be a problem if instructions are followed exactly.

E.J. Gold, *Partners in Time,*
oil on masonite, 60" x 48", 1987.

CHAPTER SEVENTEEN

FEASTING IN THE REAL WORLD

We must learn to eat by invoking life into our food and not slip into our unconscious habitual feeding in which we just transform food into fertilizer.

What does it say in the Book? It says, "He who feeds on my flesh and drinks of my blood has life eternal." We must learn from the habits of vampires which come, as you know, from the eastern European country of Transsubstantia. We must be clean when we receive bread. For this purpose we can cleanse ourselves with a special confession.

In particular a cleansing confession for preparation of ourselves to receive special bread which will soon be transsubstantiated into part of the larger Body of Christ, can be a confession of all our special, personal secrets; those little things—or sometimes big things—about ourselves we wish never to be revealed, especially to others....

When we have cleansed ourselves of bad vibrations, we are ready to take food and drink in our clean hands....

If we can see, feel and sense the Body of Christ we can bring it to life. When it lives we will feel it throbbing like a living body. The wine we drink must be warm like blood, flowing and pulsing with life.

To bring life to your bread, you must make it throb with life; see living flesh before you. Hold the bread before you, placing full attention on its form; wait until it lives before taking it into the mouth.

Do not let it die as you chew the flesh. Partake of the Body of Christ who cannot die and is forced to accept life eternal.

When we eat transsubstantiated food we force the organic body to form correspondings to digest it. This is to eat with zen. Zen monks even wait when gathering wood, to chop the body of what we call the Christ.

For those who call Him Krishna everything is Krishna; if only they knew what they really do when they eat Him. It's not sufficient to just say we eat the Body of Christ; we must make Him live, bring Him into the flesh of our food.

Do not allow the flesh to die; invoke the Holy Spirit and hold Him in your food to make living flesh...

Now drink this blood to feed the flesh as we drink milk to feed yogurt.

This is real meditation; just by the power of concentration, feeling, and sensing, we invoke life into our food and then eat it. We must learn to eat in this new way, not slip into our unconscious habitual feeding frenzy in which we transform food into fertilizer.

If this flesh and blood are really alive they should crawl down the throat, not just fall into the esophagus. This is the sacrifice which Christ really made for us and makes for us every day if we know how to take our real opportunities.

You wish to be joined to the Body of Christ? Then eat the Body of Christ and be annointed. There is truth in the idea, "We are what we eat."

Christianity was once a real school; those things we think of as trappings are the real; the things we think are most real are just the superstitious additions made by succeeding generations of idiots.

We are not ordinarily expected to be able to perform our own transsubstantiation. We are taught to depend upon a priest. But if we are to work on the essential self with the precious time we have to us, we must learn to bring our food to life so we can eat and drink every day. Everything we eat can be made part of our work if we know how to feast in the Real World.

INDEX

Sensation(s), 39
of foods, 51
organic from a corpse, 21
Sensing, 73, 104
Sex, 55
Shakespeare, 7
Sleep, 30
Solar matter, 46
Stellar cosmos, 46
St. Francis of Assisi, 15

Thinking cap, 18
Transformation, 2, 55, 86, 99 ff.
Transmutation, 47, 86
Transsubstantiation, 44, 49, 86
Triplicity, the, 1
Types (Typicality), 107
alchemical blending, 95

diagnosis of, 72
manifestations of, 8
scent of, 100
science of, 10
work, 10

Unity, non-identified
impartial, 18

Voyagers, 5

Will
force of, 18
of presence, 1
organic, 15
Work, the, 13, 33, 64, 70, 81-82, 105-106
language of, 53
Work community, 8
Work wishing, 13

Zen, 112

ABOUT THE AUTHOR

E.J. Gold is a true voyager in the heroic tradition, always keeping the highest aims and the purest ethics close to his heart throughout his explorations. His life story is a veritable odyssey through contemporary society, an adventurous journey to unlock inner secrets which he learned to communicate skillfully to others.

Mr. Gold had what could only be called a "culturally privileged" childhood in the sense that his parents' New York apartment was a meeting place of the New York intelligentsia of the time who gathered with his father Horace L. Gold, founding editor of *Galaxy* (science fiction) magazine. As a young child he met visionary writers, artists and scientists. With an early penchant for writing and all the arts, he began—as a teenager—to publish science fiction stories, to write film scripts and to work with his father on *Galaxy* magazine.

A gifted painter and sculptor, Gold moved to Los Angeles in the late 50's, studied art and cinema there, and emerged in the '60's as a respected sculptor in the California Nine group. In Hollywood, he wrote scripts for movies and television shows and performed in his own right as a comedian and a dramatic actor. With a lively interest in classical and jazz music, he professionally produced and engineered records for several major artists during the lively '60's, and he sat in with many bands in New York and Los Angeles jazz clubs.

Versatile and talented as he was, E.J. Gold was not satisfied to settle into a safe niche as a successful artist. He worked to master every art and communication field he could get his hands on, always using one form to complement his knowledge in another form—culminating in his impressive success in penetration of the subject of personal transformation. Beginning in the late '50's, he worked with people in group situations to research and test the entire range of approaches to transformation.

Having begun before spiritual life was big business, E.J. Gold is still, twenty-five years later, working actively in this field. He is now internationally known as an originator of contemporary processes of transformational psychology—a teacher's teacher—and as a masterful proponent of proven ancient methods of "labyrinth voyaging" and voluntary evolution. A writer's writer as well, he's a longtime member of SFWA (Science Fiction Writers of America), a master of satire and author of more than twenty books on subjects ranging from natural childbirth and conscious dying to shamanism and techniques of mystical vision.

According to colleagues, fans and reviewers of Mr. Gold's books, his latest series, beginning with *The Human Biological Machine as a Transformational Apparatus,* is his most significant contribution to date to the literature of mysticism, consciousness and meditation. His literary specialty is the practical use of long-atrophied classics, masterpieces of ideas presented with the utmost force and clarity, ideas not spun from intellectual abstraction but tested, lived and communicated from the heart.

With *The Seven Bodies of Man* and *Visions in the Stone,* he is taking a step causing many of his students to gasp by releasing in public format—no longer as privately-issued small-group study materials—the most sensational and profound of his discoveries over twenty-five years of research on inner awakening and transformation. Closer than ever before to the pearl-beyond-price, the heart's understanding of the never-truly-lost knowledge of life's purpose, E.J. Gold invites discerning readers everywhere to sample the banquet of his new books and take whatever they can use for their own nourishment.

FOR FURTHER STUDY

Books by E.J. Gold

Practical Work on Self
Visions in the Stone: Journey to the Source of Hidden Knowledge
American Book of the Dead
The Human Biological Machine as a Transformational Apparatus
Life in the Labyrinth
Creation Story Verbatim
The Invocation of Presence
Secret Talks on Voluntary Evolution
The Joy of Sacrifice

Books by Other Authors

Self-Completion: Keys to the Meaningful Life
    by Robert S. de Ropp
The Dream Assembly by Zalman Schachter-Shalomi
    and Howard Schwartz
Living God Blues by Lee Lozowick
The Golden Buddha Changing Masks:
    Essays on the Spiritual Dimension of Acting by Mark Olsen

Talk of the Month

A journal of work ideas featuring transcriptions of lectures by E.J. Gold. For subscription and back issue information write to Gateways.

Spoken Word Audio

Inner Awakening and Transformation
The Rembrandt Tape
The Cogitate Tape by John Lilly, M.D., and E.J. Gold

Music from E.J. Gold, the Hi-Tech Shaman

Shaman Ritual I: 'Way Beyond the Veil
Shaman Ritual II: Golden Age
Shaman Ritual III: Ritual of the Cave
Mystical Journey of the Hi-Tech Shaman
Live at the Philharmonic I
Live at the Philharmonic II
Live at the Philharmonic III
Spacing Out

Music by Other Gateways Recording Artists

Good Vibes The Jeff Spencer Trio with Bob Bachtold
Childhood's End The Jeff Spencer Trio with Tony Dey
Fourth Dawn The Jeff Spencer Trio with Tony Dey
School Days The Jeff Spencer Trio with Tony Dey
Life in the Labyrinth by Jimmi Accardi
The Wheel by Martin Silverwolf
Where You Are by Drew Kristel and the Not Always
    North American Drum Core

Video

The Movements Series
G. en Amerique
Hooray for Hollywood
Revenge of the Fly
Godfan
An Evening Shot to Hell with Parker Dixon

Dear Reader of *The Seven Bodies of Man:*

As with the other books listed for further study, this book by E.J. Gold is not presented to you as the final wisdom of the ages, but rather as a map or a formulary for alchemical practice. To quote an old punch line: How do you get to Carnegie Hall? *Practice! Practice!* For those already working with these ideas, *The Seven Bodies of Man* expands the understanding, refines some concepts for daily use, and penetrates new chambers for experimental voyaging in the labyrinth beyond mechanical life.

If this book is your first contact with this approach to transformational work, you will find the earlier books in the series helpful since they lay the groundwork and introduce the basic principles of this work. Gateways will issue in the future further volumes from the writings of E.J. Gold that have been circulated only privately to students in contact with the Worldwide Work Circle.

There is also a training program available for the basic skills of Being attention necessary to carry out any of the exercises and experiments recommended by E.J. Gold and other teachers. The Institute (IDHHB, Inc.) offers this training by correspondence, and it is workable no matter where you live or what your lifestyle, with few exceptions. The only initial requirement is that you have a minimal setup of audio playback equipment.

For information on the training program, current catalogs of study materials including audio and video, or direction on a study program tailored to your situation and degree of preparation, write or call Gateways at the address and phone listed below.

Gateways Books and Tapes
P. O. Box 370 - SB
Nevada City, CA 95959
(916) 477-1116
FAX: (916) 265-4321